My Science Library

I Can Prove It!
Investigating Science

by Kelli Hicks

Science Content Editor:
Shirley Duke

Rourke
Educational Media

rourkeeducationalmedia.com

Teacher Notes available at
rem4teachers.com

Science Content Editor: Shirley Duke holds a bachelor's degree in biology and a master's degree in education from Austin College in Sherman, Texas. She taught science in Texas at all levels for twenty-five years before starting to write for children. Her science books include *You Can't Wear These Genes, Infections, Infestations, and Diseases, Enterprise STEM, Forces and Motion at Work, Environmental Disasters,* and *Gases.* She continues writing science books and also works as a science content editor.

www.rourkeeducationalmedia.com

Photo credits: Cover © fotohunter, Keo, Anthonycz, Petr Vaclavek; Pages 2/3 © Richard Griffin; Pages 4/5 © luchschen, Marsan; Pages 6/7 © Goodluz, SUPERCOMPUTER IMAGE, Jeekc; Pages 10/11 © DELTA ROCKET IMAGE; Pages 12/13 © michaeljung; Pages 14/15 © gresei; Pages 16/17 © Richard Griffin, PRILL Mediendesign und Fotografie, Anthonycz; Pages 18/19 © Christian Lopetz Pages 20/21 © Rocket400 Studio, Christian Lopetz

Editor: Jeanne Sturm

My Science Library series produced by Nicola Stratford Designs, Florida for Rourke Educational Media.

Library of Congress PCN Data

Hicks, Kelli
 I Can Prove It! Investigating Science / Kelli Hicks
    p. cm. -- (My Science Library)
 ISBN 978-1-61810-111-2 (Hard cover) (alk. paper)
 ISBN 978-1-61810-244-7 (Soft cover)
 Library of Congress Control Number: 2011943574

Rourke Educational Media
Printed in the United States of America,
North Mankato, Minnesota

rourkeeducationalmedia.com

customerservice@rourkeeducationalmedia.com • PO Box 643328 Vero Beach, Florida 32964

Table of Contents

Prove It!

Have you ever wondered how things work? **Scientists** conduct experiments every day to try to solve problems and answer questions. They observe how different chemicals react to each other and what happens when they test a **hypothesis**, or an idea, about how something works. Scientists are always working to prove it! But how do they do it?

Scientists are careful to protect the results of their experiments by wearing gloves and keeping their work spaces clean.

An agronomist is a food scientist. This type of scientist studies soil and how the environment affects growing crops.

How Did They Prove It?

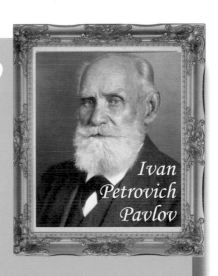

Ivan Petrovich Pavlov

Ivan Petrovich Pavlov (1849-1936) wanted to find out about the reactions of people and animals to a stimulus. He experimented with how dogs reacted to a bell ringing to signal meal time. He discovered that dogs could be trained to associate the sound of the bell with the delivery of the food. His work has helped many researchers study behavior.

5

Science is all about facts. Scientists search for relationships between a cause and the effect that follows. They develop tests to determine which factors change the outcome of an experiment and how the results are changed. They measure their results, collect **data**, and repeat the experiment to ensure it is **valid**.

Scientists who study the environment collect water samples and record the information on a computer.

How do computers help scientists collect, store, and retrieve so much information? The National Energy Research Scientific Computing Center (NERSC) has a supercomputer that collects data from many different resources. It organizes the information into one database. By doing this, it makes it easy for researchers to quickly locate results from many different studies. This helps them make better decisions about their own experiments.

Supercomputers provide information to organizations and researchers across the world.

How Did They Prove It?

Jane Goodall

Jane Goodall wanted to learn about chimpanzees in the wild. When she was 26 years old, she left her home in England and traveled to Tanzania to study chimp behavior. She used a pair of binoculars and a simple notebook to record her findings. Over time, Jane learned about chimp behavior and she was able to share her knowledge with the rest of the world.

The Scientific Method

Scientists follow specific steps to develop a plan that tests an idea. They call the process the **scientific method**. You might use the same steps if you are working on a science fair project or an experiment for school. The method is based on the ability to observe and measure the results.

How Did They Prove It?

Jonas Salk (1914-1995) was a researcher who studied diseases. He wanted to improve the vaccine available for the flu and also to develop a vaccine to prevent polio. The number of people who had polio was increasing, and the disease caused lasting damage to the body. He combined the ideas of several other researchers and developed a vaccine from a dead version of the polio virus. He tested the vaccine on himself and his family first to show his faith in the effectiveness of the vaccine.

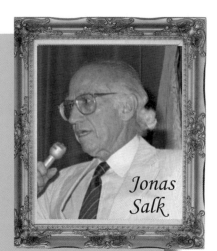

Jonas Salk

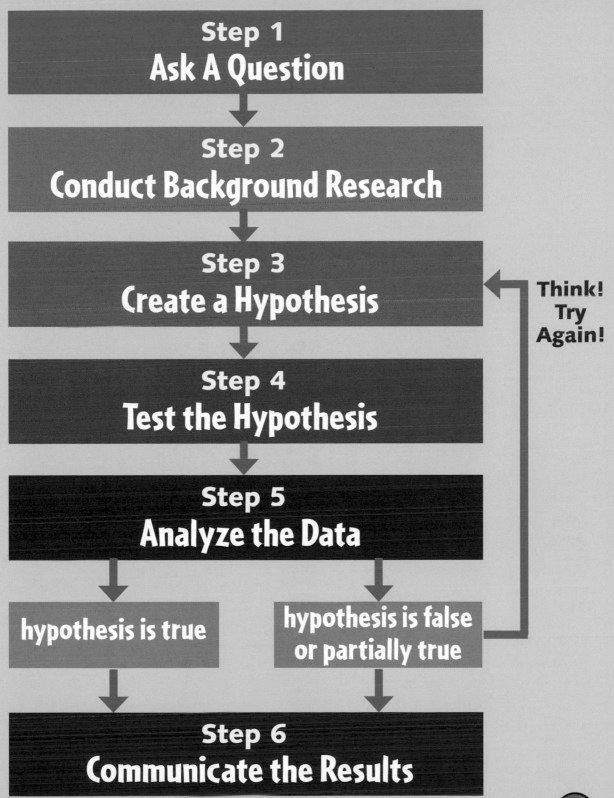

How Did They Prove It?

Dr. Robert H. Goddard (1882-1945) is considered the father of rocketry because of his contributions to the development of rocket fuels. Dr. Goddard wanted to know how to create something that would be able to launch into space and eventually touch the surface of Mars. He used information about the laws of science and tested his ideas.

Robert H. Goddard and the frame of his most famous invention, the liquid-fueled rocket.

The modern Delta Rocket is an unmanned craft used to launch satellites into space.

Ask a Question

The scientific method starts with a question about something observable. Will a particular medication treat the symptoms of a disease? How long does it take a metal object to melt? How high does the temperature have to be? The results must be **measurable**. Once the question is asked, it is time to gather information about the topic.

Step 1
Ask A Question

How does the amount of water affect the growth of a plant?

11

Research

Scientists perform **research** for many reasons. They want to find out if someone else has tested the same idea before. If there are previously recorded results, they might want to think about how to change the **variables** to see if they get a different result.

They use the Internet, the library, and even discussions with other scientists to find out if someone else has asked their question and what problems might exist with the study.

Scientists conduct research using the Internet to find out background information about a topic of study.

Scientists from around the world benefit from working together. By sharing ideas, new technology can be developed faster and be made available to more countries in the world. The World Congress in Science, Computer Engineering, and Applied Computing (WORLDCOMP) meets yearly to discuss developments in science and computers. The World Science Forum for the Twenty-First Century meets every two years to talk about developments in science research and their impact on the world society. When scientists meet to share their ideas, they learn from each other. They are also able to help each other work through problems. This helps improve the quality of research.

Step 2
Conduct Background Research

Find information about how plants grow. What have other researchers learned about watering plants, and what problems did they find with their studies?

Create a Hypothesis

Based on research, a scientist develops a hypothesis. To make an educated guess about how something works, the scientist creates a statement that shows cause and effect. **If I do this, then something else will happen.**

Remember, the results have to be measurable, and they need to answer your original question.

Example of cause and effect:
If I sprinkle salt on an ice cube, it will melt faster.

How Did They Prove It?

In 1752, Benjamin Franklin (1706-1790) used an experiment with a key and a kite to show that lightning is a form of electricity. At the time, many homes were destroyed by fires caused by lightning.

Ben Franklin invented a lightning rod. He attached a tall rod to a house. He attached a cable to the lower end of the rod and then buried it under the ground. Franklin proved that the rod could catch the electrical charge, send it down under the ground via the cable, and prevent a great number of fires.

Step 3
Create a Hypothesis

If you provide a plant with more water, the plant will grow faster.

Test the Hypothesis

In order to test the hypothesis, an experiment needs to be completed. The experiment will give information about whether the hypothesis was true or false. Scientists call the elements that do not change during an experiment the **controlled variables**. The element that does change during the experiment is the **manipulated variable**.

In our experiment, the plant, pot, and soil will be the controlled variables. The amount of water will be the manipulated variable.

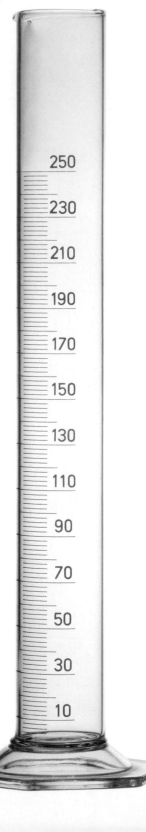

It is important to change only one element for the results to be valid. If an experiment had many manipulated variables, it would be hard to decide which variable caused the results. Scientists keep a log, journal, graph, or chart to record their observations.

Scientists graph their data to be able to compare the results easily.

Step 4
Test the Hypothesis

Water four of the plants 20 mL, 40 mL, 80 mL, or 100 mL once every day. Water the remaining plants 20 mL, 40 mL, 80 mL, or 100 mL twice every day. Measure the plants daily to determine which amount of water has the desired effect of best plant growth.

17

Analyze the Data and Draw a Conclusion

After the experiment is complete, it is time to look at the evidence and organize the data. By examining the results, the researcher can conclude whether the hypothesis proves to be true or false. Either way, it is important to redo the experiment. If repeated experiments produce the same results, researchers can consider the results to be valid.

Once scientists have proven a hypothesis true through repeated trials, it can be called a **theory**.

Number of times watered per day	Effect of different amounts of water on the height of a plants growth (mm)				
	20 mL	40 mL	60 mL	80 mL	100 mL
Once	305	365	415	435	395
Twice	425	465	415	160	85

Plants are given a specific amount of water every day and the results of their growth are recorded and studied.

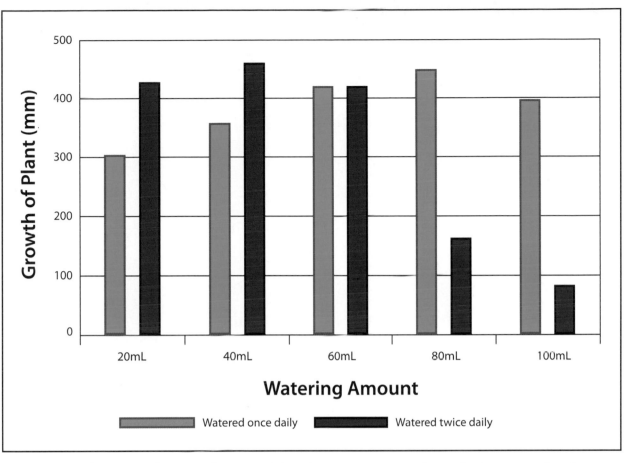

A bar graph scan be used to show a comparison between plants watered once and twice every day.

Step 5
Analyze the Data

Collect all the information from your observations, and organize the information to show the results. What do the results tell you about the relationship between watering plants and plant growth?

Communicate the Results

After spending the time looking for an answer to a question, it is important to share the results. A student might use a display board and post the results in a science fair or share them in a class presentation.

Scientists also share their results. They might publish their findings in a scientific journal or present the information to other scientists to encourage further research.

Although the steps are listed in order, it is important to remember that at any point in the process, scientists might need to back up and repeat a step or even change their original idea.

Problem

Hypothesis

Materials

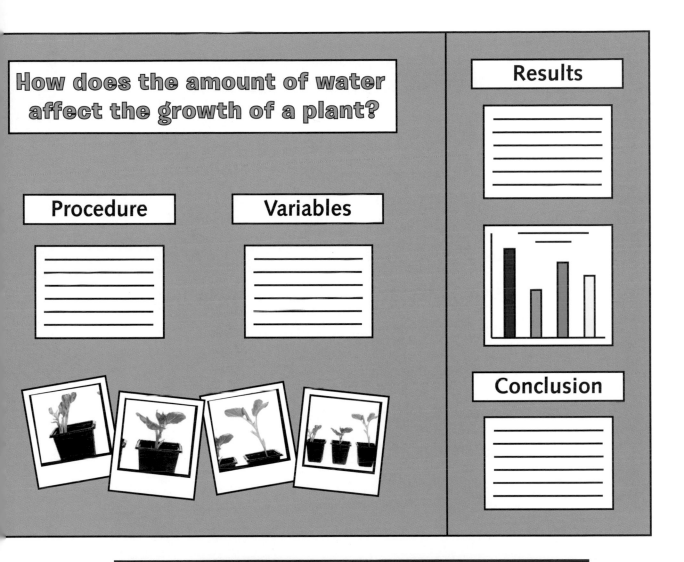

How does the amount of water affect the growth of a plant?

Procedure

Variables

Results

Conclusion

Step 6
Communicate the Results

It can be determined that the hypothesis is partially true. The research raises the question that too much water might slow the growth of a plant. It is time for more research or another study!

Show What You Know

1. When you investigate a science topic, how will you prove it?

2. What information does a scientist need to develop a hypothesis?

3. How would you explain the steps of the scientific method?

controlled variables (kuhn-TROHLD VAIR-ee-uh-buhlz): also known as dependent variables, the items that remain constant in an experiment

data (DAY-tuh): the information or the facts collected

hypothesis (hye-POTH-uh-siss): a temporary prediction that can be tested about how a scientific experiment will turn out

manipulated variable (muh-NIP-yuh-lay-tuhd VAIR-ee-uh-buhl): also known as the independent variable, the part of the experiment that is changed in the experiment

measurable (MEHZ-ur-uh-buhl): the ability to find out the size, weight, capacity, or other information about something

research (ri-SURCH): to study and find out about a topic or subject

scientific method (sye-uhn-TIF-ik METH-uhd): a method of research in which a question is asked, data is gathered, a hypothesis is created and tested, and a conclusion is reached

scientists (SYE-uhn-tists): experts who study the nature of the physical world by testing, experimenting, and measuring

theory (THIHR-ee): an idea or statement that explains how or why something happens

valid (VAL-id): sensible, based on facts and evidence

variables (VAIR-ee-uh-buhlz): items in an experiment capable of being changed

Index

Websites to Visit

www.biology4kids.com/files/studies_scimethod.html
www.uga.edu/srel/kidsdoscience/kidsdoscience-fun.htm
www.sciencefairadventure.com

About the Author

Kelli Hicks loves to read, write, and ask questions about how things work. She lives in Tampa, Florida, with her two children, Barrett and Mackenzie, her husband, and her golden retriever Gingerbread.

Ask The Author!
www.rem4students.com